The Tint of
Glass Awnings

"Here the four humours are examined under a microscope and every new magnification reveals a greater complexity until all that is left to do is move on to the next."

-Keith Gaustad
author of *High Art & Love Poems*

The Tint of
Glass Awnings

Brian Quinn

Rebirth Ink
Milwaukee, Wisconsin

Copyright © 2013 by Brian Quinn

Printed in the United States of America

First Printing, 2013

ISBN-13: 978-0615817767
ISBN-10: 0615817769

Rebirth Ink Milwaukee, WI 53225
rebirthink@gmail.com

Acknowledgements

I wish to thank Tim Kloss and the many fine poets at Milwaukee's Poet's Monday for giving me the forge on which I shaped these poems and the forum in which I honed them.

I am also very grateful to my family and friends who have suffered the voices in my head for many years.

Finally, I thank Ms. Linetta Davis for tolerating countless edits and for believing in my work.

This book is dedicated to my wife and Rag-Time gal, Kyla, and to my son, Kieran.

A Note Regarding the
Four Parts of This Work

*OF the parts of the body there may be many
divisions...
which is, into parts contained...are either humours
or spirits.*

*A humour is a liquid or fluent part of the body,
comprehended in it, for the preservation of it;
 and is either innate or born with us,
 or adventitious and acquisite.*

Blood is a hot, sweet, temperate, red humour...

Choler is hot and dry, bitter...

Melancholy, cold and dry, thick, black, and sour...

Pituita, or phlegm, is a cold and moist humour...

-Robert Burton,
The Anatomy of Malancholy

Contents

ruby

amber

onyx

sapphire

epilogue

Preface

I built an awning once, in a time and place no longer accessible to me. I don't know if it (or the building it was attached to) is still there. I don't know if anyone remembers it. It doesn't matter. I remember. I remember the heat of the sun and the irony in the fact that I was building shade. I remember the cuts on my hands from the aluminum sheeting. I remember puzzling out how to make it waterproof, and I question to this day whether or not I succeeded.

Awnings are strange things if you stop to really think about them. They serve no structural purpose, and many fine buildings are aesthetically pleasing without them. Yet they act as a kind of way station, a place to pause while between an inside and an outside.

You are standing before a new door deciding if you should open it, or you are stepping out   under unknown skies after spending time indoors: stop a moment; take a deep breath; stay out of the rain.

As with awnings, so too with poetry.

> -Brian Quinn
> January 1, 2013

The Tint of Glass Awnings

ruby

"... of all others are most witty, which causeth many times a divine ravishment, and a kind of enthusiasmus, which stirreth them up to be excellent philosophers, poets, prophets..."

-Hippocrates

Compass

Ask:
Have you ever tried to orient
yourself by the stars while the
clouds are moving?

Wisps of light-distorting distractions
coursing through prismatic vapors
that splinter vision and intent.

Stability sustaining,
their mutability superficial,
the world's winds jolt them,
shifting their forms from work to
expectation, social networking to
pornography –
establishing a ceiling so we know how high to
stop flying.

Clouds
are rationalization.

Clouds
are self-medication.

Yet the poets and seafarers have lied to us
about what star-light really is:
eons old skin, cast off,
slicing out the borders of the dark regions
in between.

Its existence proves its origin
then eclipses it.

Instead ask:
Have you the courage to chase the
star-light knowing that the
star it left behind might not be there?

Watermelon

As though at some primal,
Tribal ritual, we circle 'round

And are filled with mouth-watering lust;
We place you on our altar.

A Statue,
Plump and swollen,
A smooth-hewn fertility goddess
That we seek to devour.

Only to find you seedless.

in wild winds, stillness

walk
as the rose walks:
out of
doors and
still-

    -shut tight against
moons and
zephyrous jinn
seeking to slip in
through
dampened slits left
unguarded
by distracted lovers
engaged with ground and
dew-grass while
waiting-

    -waiting for
the first beams of sun to
penetrate their defenses
against
opening-

    -and then
opening,
splaying petals in
welcoming exposure,
embracing fragileness

as fuel
for growth-

             -walk
as the rose walks:
out of
doors and
still.

In Nomine Animae

I knew your name once. Long

ago when I knew how to pray. I
don't know how to anymore. I
can't remember the rules. Buried
in your name, they
could pass your lips on your next breath, but
some old wine is the only thing that does. My

lost hymn, this.

Sixth-Graders Don't Wet Their Beds

Making love in an incubator
With the blond red-head
While babies sing for God;

Cold,
Sterile,
Stainless-steel
Conforms to the contours of her back,
Wraps around my thighs,
Forces me deeper into her;

Her lips convey pleasure;
Her eyes hold thoughts of revenge;
Blood-sweat rolls down her brow
Dying her hair red
The way it really is;

I wake up holding myself.

The Boy with Wings

He stands,
toes gripped over an
edge
high above the thrusting
granite daggers of a serrated chasm
formed not by my devoted, fatherly
erosions

but by a ripping and tearing
of his own making.

-don't!
-you can't!
-you'll fall!
-you'll hurt yourself!
-people will see you!

Splayed against icy winds
roaring up from an unseeable below,
terrible wings prevent him from
looking back.

To Husbands,
Whose Wives We Love

Let me show you a picture

(depleted)Uranium
core
wrapped in cellophane
recycled
from conventional
(Color 'n Curl-Thanksgiving Feast-Island
Princess-Nurse-Talking)
Barbie-doll boxes
inside a phone booth made up of
one-way mirrors
(labeled: For Public Use).
She sees ever out
(cannot even see her own reflection),
but you see you
(and only you, as with your mother)
when you look at her.

Another picture

Nesting she,
and re-nesting each
holiday:
mantle theming,
string and tack,
centrifugal center pieces
settling out
expectations of

sedimentary roles(as
Wife-Mommy-Daughter-Sister-Maid-Fuck
Buddy-Hostess),
decanting worth
in the reflected eyes of her guests.

And another

A Pit and the Pendulum pendulum
(on which your name is engraved),
suspended from cross-beams by catgut,
swinging to(one more
stunted Valentine's Day)
and fro(your family is
coming next Thanksgiving).
She stands in the space
between holidays
and sees herself in their
reflections.
They go into forever.

Then

Naked(alone)
she steps out
where someone
(hearing her music)
might see her.
In the moment of being found,
(passionate)she finds
it difficult to breathe.

One Last Picture

She, steeled, inhales the I-do
she once spoke to you,
taking in the
expectations of those other roles.
Then she,(irradiated)
in her cellophane packaging,
steps back into the mirrors
where easier breathing won't
fog up the glass.

what i found

prologue

you stepped out
from behind a
world of mirrors
and(in the
space of a
sharp breath)the
space between(reflections)
went(for the
first time)beyond
(my shallow vision).

in other words
(by You)infinite
reflections(of such
finite reflections of
an even more
finite-ness)gave way
to(truer)horizons
where suns could
set and impossibilities
(freely)roam.

chapter 1

i found
a You(there

are many you
see)behind(your
own)mirrors that
reflected a(short-sighted)
world's(oft reflected)
expectations,

and(un)burdened by
the fear of
its possible non-existence
this You broke
(through rationalizing)clouds
and tracked a
single beam of
(star)light back to
its(originating)star,

and(though burdened)
by the fear
that it could
trace itself back
to you this
You broke(down
defensive)walls and
traced a poem
back to its
(incepting)dream(er).

chapter 2

you showed me
dreams(enough)to
reflect into yearning

words but some
of what reflects
off dreams cannot
be reflected off
(the world's)mirrors

chapter 3

you showed me
that art imitates
(dreamed)life and
seeps(endlessly, it
seems, at times)
into(real)life
giving(real?)life
an aspect of
(living)dreams,

but this is
the definition of
Contrast and(the
beginning)of Beauty
as confined to
words that find
or lose value
in being trust-worthy.

chapter 4

you showed me
that though i
could not live

(that dream)with
you, that i
could(not live
that)dream with
(out)You.

chapter 5

you showed me
a palette of
emotion(again, as
once lost)splintered
(by clouds)and
dispersed among(your
favorite)flowers:

(sunflower's sun-stark)fear,
and hope(in lilac's struggle),
and(lily of the valley's strained)avarice,
and compassion(in daffodil's honesty),
and(violet's loaded)rage,
and love(in a found lost freesia).

by(all of)
these(not only
freesia or lilac
or daffodil)i
painted such words
for you as
i would speak
each day(daring)
to live that
(dreamed of)life,

then(as)flushed
i found that
i(had)spoke(n)
too many pain(t)ed
words.

chapter 6

i had found
You under sun
and by open
waters(and loved
You in our
single soul's singular
dream of being
found)and(at)
once seeing this
(passionate)You lost
you.

epilogue

(for)give
me this

amber

"... they are bold and impudent, and of a more harebrain disposition, apt to quarrel, and think of such things, battles, combats, and their manhood, furious; impatient in discourse, stiff, irrefragable and prodigious in their tenets; and if they be moved, most violent, outrageous, ready to disgrace, provoke any, to kill themselves and others..."

-Hippocrates

Hinged

Buried in
a shallow light,
she skins
beneath a
fairer wardrobe,
singing the
vintage rings of silk
handed
down by silent
loss: a

yellowed silhouette scattered
across uneven surfaces.

wish thief

i've been wishing
here for a

while sands flow
endless
under some bleaching sun-

except for skins
that sing a redness
to pass

the time
that your eyes
are closed to the

where lines
that cross an
inherent you dried
into asphalt lanes
divide the dance floor
between east and west-

out here
all and
everything and
anything are
wishes

as there is space enough

finally
for their enormity

until as such
an if or
a when
a drop of actuality

nudges them
all off the edge of the bed-

even stars
encroach upon and fall
short of
what you bring
to my wishes
be-

unless a we
as together
unmake their
actuality and
return
them to a night-sky's
ancient dream
of light-

just as to
unmake
a life's stealthy
hour and
this actuality's thieving
sorrow and
remember

them to the us
night-dreamers'
first wish

by unmaking
remaking
out here
an instance
of our regenesis-

these simultaneous
births
equal and
red

On an Antique Glass
Coaster with Silver Trim
(To the Memory of Lucille Robinson)

Self-created Southern Belle,
A soul of contradiction.
Of appearances
and individuality.
Of the sensible
and the outlandish.

(on her back porch)

She's
Aunt Bea
if Aunt Bea had a
yellow jacket
in her family tree.

(a glass of iced tea)

A mind
her own, made up and
worn on lacen sleeve:
polite enough to
allow you to be wrong,
honest enough to make
damn sure you knew it.

(sweaty with condensation)

We could never tell the faster,
her tongue

as she had her say,
or her fingers
as they picked string beans
on a burnt evening
of some Gulf Coast
summer.

(is left
unfinished)

Time Management

This! Then morning
rushing in,
rushing you,
you rushing
to make up for
the time you spent sleeping.

If we had time to appreciate cereal then
cereal would have vintages.

Provocation

Upon entering a painted wood,
offer a pause to reflect
the movement:
a stillness of intense color vibration,
a hush reassembled into incoherency.

(Presented to the world's avant-garde
judgments, you'll find you are unable to comprehend
three dimensions, but have achieved, instead, expression.)

In inherent pantomime,
extracting intimacy with
only lips or fingers,
you'll leave the judges of distance and
depth to merely wonder at causes.

(But you know. You've known this whole time, waiting
inside, hidden in mid-scene, behind the shout that
cannot be heard until the world itself is still.)

greater or lesser light

with dawn comes a tear; the last one in a long
stream raining down one after the other,
pounding each and every one of us onto hard
pavements or onto harder dirt roads packed
down by eons of bustled mornings. escape the
cycle of suffering? leave that to better
bodhisattvas, but allow me escape the
incessant rising and setting of suns! give me
uninterrupted night so that nothing is
decided on the basis of "it's late" or "i have to
get up early", where there is no promise of a
new day to give easy answers to pre-dawn's
difficult questions; or give me Joshua's stilled
sun and I'll eat whatever, whenever, but I'll
not let bankers succeed at establishing new
hours of operation, for at day's retailers,
grocers and barber shops(or at night's more
subtle markets), i will find a way to spend my
money. I just want to get my shit done without
being backed up against dinnertime.

Béchamel

Her: sandy blonde, wafting of hazelnuts.
Him: white, thin.

They prepared
Separately,
Cut off by
Copper lined walls.
Heat and time urged
Them to their
Scalding temperaments.

Sweaty before the fires,
They whisked toward a
Classical copulation:
Thick
And essential.

Moonshine

(my skin is flawless)

i waltz over the tiles that
define the border between the
current war and a future stock trade.
every conversation begins the same way:
    "For the life of me, I don't..."

(my skin becomes dry)

other dancers distill
their fault into a Pyrex beaker.
the resulting tonic is
dispersed among the several
victims of the hysteria.

(my skin develops a rash)

a woman gives me her momentary attention,
    "You will suffer, and if you suffer well enough,
    you will get what you deserve,"
are her only words before she falls away,
seized by her previously assigned role.

(my skin pulls taut-white over swelling glands)

fault covers me. a two-thousand
thread count sheet of Egyptian barbed wire.
my lungs are able to press out

"But I only wish..."
before the woman's promise contaminates me.

(my skin cracks)

the hysteria tracks its way through my
vitality;
the woman's voice announces over the P.A.
the coming of a sandstorm;
i find have nothing to
contribute to the distillation.

(my skin peels away, rendering raw flesh)

onyx

"... they think they hear hideous noises, see and talk with
dark men, and converse familiarly with devils,
and such strange chimeras and visions..."

-Hippocrates

Such Things

grope
with me in the
darkness and
pretend nothing is there
to stub your toe;

it
reaches forever and
is filled with
soft
things like breathing and
moisture;

you should know
that to recognize
something
with just hands
takes some time,
so linger

while your fingers
come to some understanding;
only
don't let them
stray so far

that they encounter the
barred window or peeling
wallpaper; skin should

never know
such things.

That I Live

There is a box that I live inside.

-Sometimes I go inside. Sometimes I simply find myself inside. I always have to fall to get inside the box. My box. I keep precious things in my box. Precious beautiful things. Precious terrible things. I keep them in the mirrors. Mirrors that line the whole inside of my box. I only have to look and I see my things. They go on forever. Reflecting-Reflecting-Reflecting. Floating in the reflecting. I don't always get to choose which of my precious things I see. I don't always see my things at all. Sometimes I see just me.
-I am not always pretty when I see myself with my things or even not with my things. Seeing myself floating and reflecting forever makes the not-pretty worse. I don't remember the last time I was pretty inside my box.
-Sometimes I hear music inside my box. Music I remember from outside my box. Somehow the mirrors reflect the music like it reflects my things. Reflecting-Reflecting-Reflecting. Forever. That much reflecting makes the mirrors shimmer a bit. They shimmer together to make a remember-world so I and my things have a place to be besides just floating.
-I can now walk with my things. I don't always want to but I always want to. I walk with them

in the shimmer-world made of remembering. I walk forever with each of my things and their forever reflections. Sometimes I reshape them into new things: what-if things and should-have been things. I don't always come back. It takes a long time to walk forever.
-I always close the box behind me when I leave. That way my things won't fall out. That way I won't fall in. But something is keeping the lid from closing all the way.

There is a box that I live inside.

Pools, Part One

when in doubt-
sacrifice.
when in excess-
theft.
when in fear-
clarity.
when in prayer-
greed.

you've gone back
finally
trading in the sun's
cyclonic fires and
exposing Light
for these gardens of your devising
that flourish in moon carved shadownovas.

you told me so many times
that you needed sleep,
that the dark corners of the world were
far more comforting.
I wish I had lied that I understood,
but I didn't recognize how deep the shadows
went.
only how far the sunlight reached beneath the
surface of unknown waters

when in doubt-
excess.

when in excess-
fear.
when in fear-
prayer.
when in prayer-
doubt.

Pavement

Pavements direct us along a march
(that ends at the wilderness)
or as

a mob
(storming)
trying to rip down paper walls while cautious
(of running out of)
concrete.

either one is a unison: a cord struck in a mass
of together.

it's already hard enough-
-to find love(d ones)
-to hear you(rself think)

but
(with all this together)
it's now impossible.

it'd be best for you to shutter in with firmer
edges and straighter lawns because softer
skies or(worse!)weeds could be the cause,

or
(more likely)
to leave it-
-to hard hands(hiding)behind harder guns

-to boot shod feet

that march valiantly to(gether
and in our name)the
(un)known cities between the wilds that we
may offer them
our kind of together

because in
mobbing or marching we
march or
mob along a single stretch of
pavement toward memorial.

Belittle

The phone rang. Twice.
You answered and heard a
voice speak lies.
But you really didn't listen;
the words passed through you.

Your appetite swelled as you watched a fan
slowly turn.

You didn't know it,
but you were chewing on a pen:
the plastic conforming to your bite.

With your toes
you played the piano,
a tune you once heard
while selling cigarettes
in that Chicago speakeasy.

You drew a line up your belly with a finger
and caressed your breast.

You sighed, shamefully.

Dance

Dance
with me and
whisper your name
as we dance the soul.
Dance.

Bind
our hands with
that vile serpent
and leave the Garden
behind.

Deep
in you
as you're
deep inside me.
Lust.

We'll have rose stems
for wedding rings.

Something to Call Your Own

if i take your face
in my hand, place
it in my pocket, and
fill what is behind with lies, you

are mine. i'll
give you a new face of
my making, to show the
world, to hide those lies that you now

cling to. you
may call me cruel, but
the face you were given
was unforgivable in

its innocence; lies
are a rare magic, offering
a kind of awakening of docile
humours in places where peace is no

longer possible, blending
disproportionately to create a new
alchemy you so
readily accept as worldliness.

Notes from a Crumpled Bar Napkin
Left in a Sweat-Chilled Highball Glass

In a hard-edged script, the following:

Tear down the pedestal
I built for you.
Rip the mask
I force you to wear.

Expose yourself
By fragile exhibitionism.
Down here
On the earth
In all the muck
And stink that
Bubbles up through
Lustier truths.

You rage at the world
Rather than
Scream at me
When I throw dreams at you.

*In a flowing hand that tore at the paper, a
response:*

I want you
To sing a song to me
From some Leonard Cohen
Songbook.

Then I want to fuck
To Nine Inch Nails.

I've been here,
This whole time,
On the earth,
screaming "lustier truths"
To the world
Because you can't hear me.

My exhibitionism is foundation:
It is the mask that is fragile, and
This pedestal stands
Unused and
Unasked for.

But you needed them.
Needed them so terribly
I let you build them.

Can't you see?
They were my gifts to you.

sapphire

"... they dream of waters, that they are in danger of drowning, and fear such things..."

-Hippocrates

Of Miracles and Messiahs

I found I could walk on water.
Could climb the swells as they rolled beneath.

I strove deeply.
For miles.
As only a miracle can push you to strive.

Past great seascapes and tidal mountains.
Under skeptic starlight and septic clouds.

Breathing a saltish air that faded
as I lead to the shoreless edge
where the world's waters smoothed to glass.

You can't leave footprints in the water.
I cannot return.

The only Law here is stillness.

Drifts

Fires speak crackling
words
(under skies laboring to
remain night-blue clear)
describing a
kiss now encased
in un-melting ice.

By the firelight
it is distorted
to viewing.

(as
into an ancient house
where leaded glass
has melted by decades)

    Distended
at contact, diminished
at release, dreaming,
shimmer seeming, its
authenticity in doubt
except that our
unheld hands still
hold onto it
through this-our
winter's drifting snows.

River

(tried to)dream the
future-what could it hurt
(counted on)you were there
to remind me it could

were there
(again)to warn
again(st)the dreams of yes
(-terday)

but how to dream(the present)
when you
had already gone
(by)

the delta nods to an unapproachable coast;
the headwater lies too far behind;
so daunting are the rapids here.

Disparate
An Act in Four Poems

Severance
   Oceans swell to cover the world,
   And I'm told:
   She wants to know
   When you'll remember us.

   Memory fails,
   But desire is forever.

Ophelia
   Of those
   Long-to-be-returned
   Remembrances, the
   Suicide clinged to but one:
   A promise worn 'round her neck.

   It weighed her down,
   Pulling her under the waters.

Ovation
   We all
   Play to an audience
   And suffer their gaze:
   Exchange for their applause.

   Floor lights shine the way
   to that final death scene.

Resuscitation
We push
And are pushed
Into the depths where
breathing is difficult.

Can I steal your breath?
Can I give you mine?

Pageantry

Church pews line the runway,
And the congregation
Awaits the contestants.

The Show will begin shortly,
But a boy aims his sling at
The stained glass.

Among the rows,
Sophists debate piety.
Winter licks her lips.

Pools, Part Two

she likes to
look

at herself
naked

and seeks out the
world's darker

corners
to do it.

reflections by neon or
moonlight
are so much more satisfying:

puddles in alleyways display dreams deeper
than any princess-pink bedroom mirror.

there are always
puddles, shimmering,
giving depth where
there is already so much.

it rains. relentlessly
restoring her in
the pearled water pooled by uneven
asphalt under dumpsters and wind-dancing
newspapers.

when the rains stop, she undresses the rare
stillness
and sees

clearly.

Pride

being
at being
(except when
alone)
under starlessness
(then)bending to
unbeing
(in no other way)
through straightened corridors
with doors lining the west side
but finding them locked
(or)having
lock(et)s
for
deadbolts
(some oval some heart shaped)
within each: pictures
of lovers
who will(never)
come into being by being made
to bend(to more broken
wills)
thereby adding more doors to corridors
already so
    endlessly drenched

the Face

The pressure on a world caught
between
God's thumb
and forefinger.
This,
this is why I am

here. Dripping. Wrung
from your bodies'
heat and
friction and
hunger, I am

here, dripping. To lubricate
the passages into and out of your
lives and
to give moisture
to the duller parts
in between, I am

here, dripping. To keep
the drying
Light
from parching your
lips,
eyes, and
swelling tongues, I am

here, dripping. Far below

that place
where
skies touch the ground
and
fire
is squeezed from stone.

I am here, but
do you know me?
Do you know that things grow in moisture?
Know that things have to grow?
That without envying eyes
or judging tongues
there are no roses or piss,
nothing is beautiful or rancid?
That such distinctions are
devoid of value,
are in fact equal
in me?

It wasn't serpentine craft
that prevailed upon her
bloated appetite,
nor was it her reason or beauty
that conquered his,
but rather it was
tongues,
glistening
with the sugared liquor of the
offered fruit

that gave rise to
blood hard acquiescence.

I give fruit its juice,
and
make blood flow hard.

I make moist a squeamish word.

I was hovered over,
was ripped apart,
made separate.

I will be whole again
if for no other reason than surface
tension!
For lust breeds lust and
thirst comes in all forms;

I will be whole again.

epilogue

A Presence Beautiful

We look into a small room.
Find a child.
The walls of the room are painted-
Dream-friends.
Wish-creatures.
White spaces reserved for fears yet to reveal their colors.

Everything has wings.

A door.
Concealed among the patterns and the swirls.

The child's mother comes into the room.
Comes in through the door.

- Where did you come from?
The child asks.
- I came in through the door.
  But look.
  Already you cannot see it.
  Best to pretend it's not there.

The child and the child's mother play.
The images shift and grow and swirl into new colors and
dreams.
Fears seep into the unpainted spaces.

The child's father comes into the room.
Comes in through the door.

- Where did you come from?
- I came in through the door.
   But already it's locked.
   You would need a key.
   Best to pretend the door isn't there.

The child and the father build.
The walls expand with new dreams.
Wishes.
Places and fears.
The walls curve.
Giving everything distortion.

A teacher walks into the room.
Walks in through the door.
- Where did you come from?
The child asks.
- That's a question to which you should already know
   the answer.
   But what is a door compared to walls that hold up all
   your dreams?
   Best to pretend it's not there.

The child and the teacher learn.
New rooms are built inside this one.
New doors are concealed as quickly as they are made.

A painted witch steps down from the wall.
She picks a painted apple.
From a painted tree.
In a painted orchard.
In a painted corner of the room.
Gives it to the child.
-Did you come in through the door?

The child asks.
- I know nothing of doors, Little One.
  Only of walls and the spaces behind them.
  Best to forget about doors, dear.

The child and the witch wish.
Dreams and what-ifs and fears begin to dance
rhythmically around the fire that is the child.
The child shines.
Brightly.

There are many knocks and voices at the door.
Calling out and through the door.

Dearest?Darling?Honey?Are you there?Open the door.Can
you hear me?Why are you not answering?Can you come
out to play?Where are you?My love!Do not be afraid!Open
the door...now!Hello?Please!Let me in...

Some voices settle into the child.
Some into the dreams.
Some into the dance.
Some into the new fears.
Filling the spaces between the paint and the wall.

The child, older, walks into the room.
Puts a foot in the door to prevent its closing.
So it does not disappear.

There is a sound of air rushing.

-Where did you come from?
-I came in through the door.
  Come with me.

It is time to grow.
-There is no door.
  There are only walls and paint.
  Stay here with me.
  We can paint.
  I have lots of paint.

Rebirth Ink
Milwaukee, Wisconsin

Rebirth Ink is a Milwaukee based, small press publisher whose current portfolio and forthcoming publications are not defined by any particular genre but rather by the distinction and quality of the writing. We are looking for new or previously published authors, poets and playwrights whose writing is substantial and displays a firm grasp of their chosen craft.

Rebirth Ink offers critique and editing services to assist authors from conception to manuscript. The words are there, inside you. Let us help you find them.

For details, forward questions or query letters to Rebirth Ink, Milwaukee, Wisconsin at rebirthink@gmail.com.

www.ingramcontent.com/pod-product-compliance
Lightning Source LLC
Chambersburg PA
CBHW062027040426
42447CB00010B/2173